THE WORLD OF SCIENCE

THE INVISIBLE
WORLD

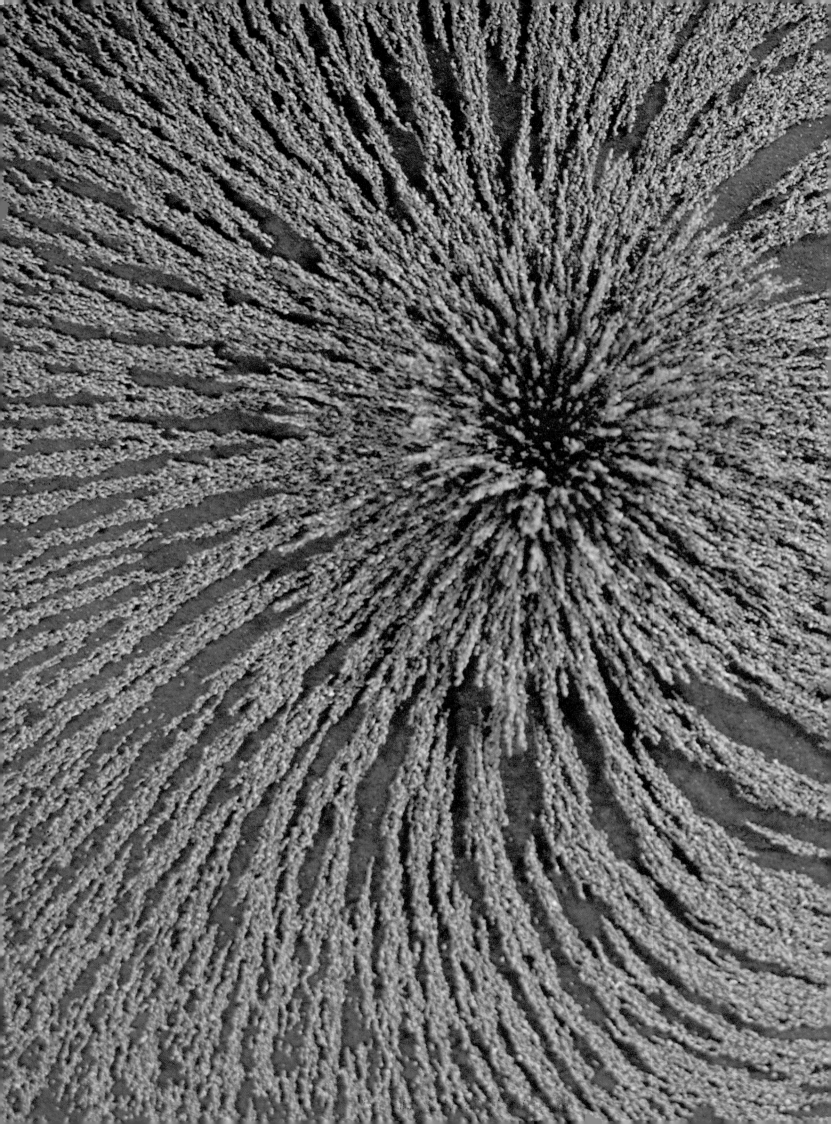

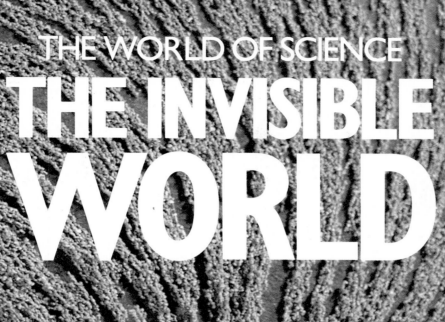

THE WORLD OF SCIENCE
THE INVISIBLE
WORLD

RON TAYLOR

Facts On File Publications
New York, New York ● Bicester, England

THE INVISIBLE WORLD

Copyright © 1985 by Orbis Publishing Limited,
London

First published in the United States of America in
1985 by Facts on File, Inc., 460 Park Avenue South,
New York, N.Y. 10016

First published in Great Britain in 1985 by Orbis
Publishing Limited, London

**Library of Congress Cataloging in Publication
Data**

Main entry under title:

World of Science

  Includes index.
  Summary: A twenty-five volume encyclopedia of
scientific subjects, designed for eight- to-twelve-year-
olds. One volume is entirely devoted to projects.
  1. Science—Dictionaries, Juvenile.   1. Science—
Dictionaries
Q121.J86   1984   500   84-1654

ISBN: 0-8160-1069-2

Printed in Italy
10 9 8 7 6 5 4 3 2 1

Consultant editors
Eleanor Felder, Former Managing Editor, *New Book
of Knowledge*
James Neujahr, Dean of the School of Education, City
College of New York
Ethan Signer, Professor of Biology, Massachusetts
Institute of Technology
J. Tuzo Wilson, Director General, Ontario Science
Centre

Previous pages
Is this an exotic
flower? No, it is the
pattern iron filings
form in response to the
magnetic field of an
ordinary horseshoe
shaped magnet.

Editor Penny Clarke
Designer Roger Kohn

CONTENTS

1 INVISIBLE MATTER

Matter and emptiness **6**
Invisible gases **8**
Gases we breathe **10**
What are liquids? **12**
Boiling, freezing and melting **14**
What are solids? **16**
Heaviest and lightest **18**
Particles, waves and rays **20**

2 HIDDEN FORCES

What is energy? **24**
Energy and force **26**
Atoms and the Universe **28**
The strongest forces **30**
Other strong forces **32**
Chemical forces **34**
Energy for life **38**
Vital body chemicals **40**

3 THINKING AND DREAMING

Brain waves and body waves **44**
Sleep and dreams **46**
Who's intelligent? **50**
All by instinct **54**
Having visions **56**
Mind power **58**

Glossary **62**
Index **64**

Note There are some unusual words in this book. They are explained in the Glossary on pages 62–63. The first time each word is used in the text it is printed in *italics*.

▲ Just up from an ice-hole, this Weddell seal is in a marvellous energy balance with nature. Its entire life is spent in or around freezing Antarctic waters, yet it keeps as warm as any other mammal.

MATTER AND EMPTINESS

What is matter? It is everything in the world that we can see, touch, feel, smell and so on. A chair, a rock, another person, a pool of water, a cloud, are all examples of matter. If there is enough light to see by, then anyone with normal sight can see any of these objects quite clearly. But if these objects, which are so visible, are examples of matter, how can matter be invisible?

Matter has structure
The examples of matter given above are very different from one another. A chair and a pool of water not only look different but feel very different – water has a much softer feel. You can hardly feel a cloud or mist at all.

Hard substances, such as the wood of the chair, are called solids. Water, with its much softer feel, is called a liquid. A cloud is called a *vapour*, which is rather similar to a gas (page 8) although it really consists of many tiny drops of water. What makes solids, liquids and gases different, even though they are all forms of matter, is their structure, the way in which they are made up of *atoms*.

The diagram shows this structure in a simple way. But no one can hope to see the structure of matter simply by looking at an object such as the chair, water or cloud. The structure of all forms of matter is, in fact, invisible to us.

Emptiness
Everywhere on Earth we find matter. Even the air we breathe, which is normally invisible except as a rustling of trees or grass, is a form of matter – it is a familiar example of a gas. Look up at the night sky, however, and you will see something quite different.

In between the stars and other bright parts of the sky such as The Milky Way, is darkness, or outer space. This darkness is mostly empty – it contains very few atoms of matter, in the forms of solids, liquids and gases.

Space or emptiness exists down here on Earth too – and everywhere else in the *Universe* where matter is found. If this sounds like a contradiction, look at the diagram once more. You can see that there is *some* empty space even between the close-packed atoms of solids. And inside the atoms themselves, as you can see on page 28, there is lots more empty space. Add it all up, and you will see that the Universe – everything that exists – is mostly nothing at all!

▼ Atoms in four states of matter. **1** In solids the atoms are held fixed in position. **2** In liquids they can move around a bit. **3** In gases the atoms move around as much as they want.

4 In plasmas, atoms break down into even smaller parts.

► Between the matter of the stars and galaxies, the Universe is mostly emptiness.

▼ Gases in air expand and contract as they are heated and cooled. Stand a bottle in hot water (top). Stretch a balloon over it (middle). Then put it in cold water. The air inside cools and contracts. The balloon is sucked in and air from outside inflates it.

► Astronaut and moon buggy are lighted up by the Sun, yet the Moon's sky looks dark. This is because it lacks air to scatter the Sun's rays and make daylight.

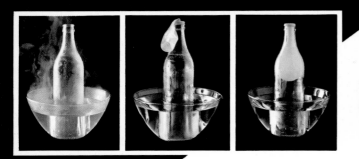

▲ The atom of hydrogen is the simplest of all atoms. It contains just two sub-atomic particles: a proton and an electron. Hydrogen also exists in two other forms, called deuterium and tritium. These have atoms that are a little more complicated. Their atoms contain an additional type of particle, the neutron. The pie chart shows that hydrogen is by far the most plentiful gas in the Universe.

isotopes of hydrogen
● electron
O proton
● neutron

INVISIBLE GASES

Gases are the thinnest and most lightweight form of matter that exists commonly here on Earth. Many gases have no colour and so are invisible too.

Out in space beyond the Earth, gases exist in much larger amounts. The stars, for example, are really huge balls of hot gas. Spaces between the stars contain cooler gases, but these are spread out very thinly indeed – an atom here, an atom there.

The lightest gases
Most lightweight of all gases is hydrogen. Stars are made mostly of hydrogen, together with some helium, the next most lightweight of gases.

The atom of hydrogen has the simplest structure of all gas atoms, and so of all forms of matter. This invisible gas exists in three rather different forms, as the diagram shows. The simplest is also by far the commonest – the ordinary hydrogen of stars and of the thin clouds of gas between them.

Common and uncommon
When hydrogen burns in stars at tremendously high temperatures, it changes into helium – which explains why these two gases are by far the most common in the whole Universe. Many other heavier kinds of gas also exist here on Earth and out in space, for example the gases of the air we breathe (page 10). The pie chart in the diagram shows that compared with hydrogen and helium all these other gases are rare in the vast spaces of the Universe – although some are quite common down here on planet Earth.

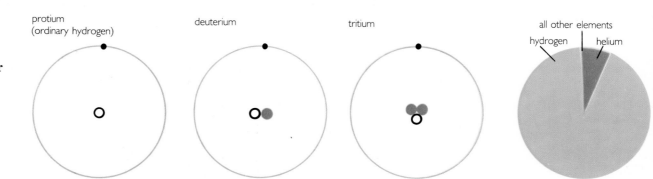

protium (ordinary hydrogen)

deuterium

tritium

all other elements
hydrogen   helium

◄ Giant airships were once filled with the lightweight gas hydrogen. This gas, however, burst into flames very easily – with disastrous results as this photograph of the crash of the Hindenberg shows. Helium, a much safer gas, is now used.

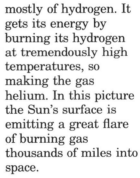

◄ The Sun is made mostly of hydrogen. It gets its energy by burning its hydrogen at tremendously high temperatures, so making the gas helium. In this picture the Sun's surface is emitting a great flare of burning gas thousands of miles into space.

▼ The Sun's outermost atmosphere, or gas layer, is called the corona. It is so thin and faint that it can only be viewed during an eclipse. This picture was taken using special photographic methods.

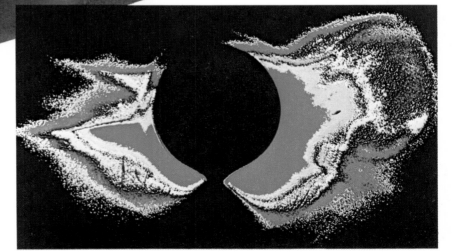

9

The labels in the image read: carbon dioxide, oxygen, carbon dioxide, carbon dioxide, carbon dioxide, carbon dioxide, nitrogen, oxygen, oxygen, nitrogen, nitrogen, oxygen, nitrogen, carbon, carbon, carbon

▲ Air contains the gases oxygen, nitrogen and carbon dioxide, which are vital to life on Earth. The picture shows their movements in Nature.

The invisible gases most familiar to us are the ones in the air that we breathe. They are the most important for our lives. Without them we, and all other forms of life, would soon cease to exist.

Vital oxygen
In every ten parts of air the gas oxygen has about two parts. It is vital to us because every living cell of our bodies needs it to stay alive. Oxygen plays an important part in the chemistry of living cells – that is, the ways in which they go on working and reproducing themselves during life.

Also, no-one would ever be able to light a useful fire without oxygen, because this is the gas that allows things to burn.

Harmless nitrogen
In every ten parts of air, nitrogen forms about eight parts. Although our bodies need nitrogen too, we get most of it from complicated nitrogen-substances in our food and not from the air. The air-nitrogen, however, is completely harmless to us, and is vital for the growth of plants, as shown in the nitrogen-cycle diagram.

Airy movements
The diagram above shows how oxygen, nitrogen and other air gases move around from the air to the bodies of animals and plants and back again.

Another gas that is vital to life but in much smaller amounts than oxygen and nitrogen, is carbon dioxide. This is a gas that we and other animals breathe out. But, even more importantly, it is the gas that green plants breathe in and use to build up their bodies.

In this way, plants feed on air, together with salts in the soil. Now we and other animals feed on plants, or on other animals that have fed on plants. So the invisible air gases are the very basis of life on Earth.

Oxygen, besides being so vital to our body chemistry, also protects us against the more harmful rays of the Sun. High

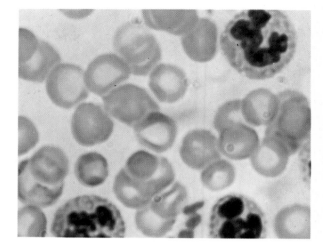

▲ Blood cells magnified more than a thousand times. The smaller cells, or red blood cells, are the ones that carry the oxygen that is vital to feed our body tissues.

up in the Earth's air or atmosphere, oxygen is changed by these harmful *ultraviolet rays* into another gas called ozone. This then stops the rays getting through to the Earth's surface to do damage to our bodies.

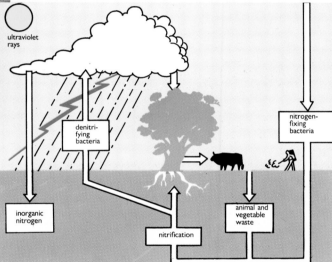

▲ How nitrogen moves around in Nature. Mostly, this is the work of microscopic bacteria in the soil and in plant roots.

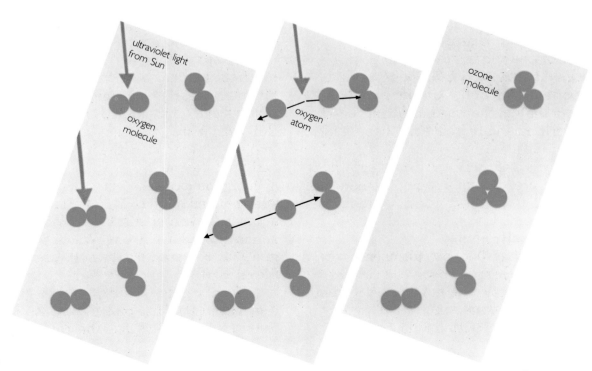

◀ High up in the Earth's atmosphere or air, the gas oxygen turns into the gas ozone. The diagram shows how this happens.

WHAT ARE LIQUIDS?

A gas, if it is not kept sealed in a closed container – such as a balloon – will spread out more and more thinly because its atoms or *molecules* are not attracted to one another enough to keep the gas in one place. A molecule can be either just one atom of a substance, or a number of atoms stuck together.

A liquid, on the other hand, will stay put in an open container, such as a bowl – if this is the right way up! The molecules of the liquid are closer together than those of the gas, so they attract one another more and bind the liquid together. And that is why the liquid stays more or less in one place.

Curious liquid habits
This binding-together of liquid molecules can have some curious effects. Above the surface of a liquid, say, water in a bowl, there are no more water molecues to bind to – and so the surface molecules bind all the more strongly to one another. You may have noticed a fly or other small insect struggling on the surface of some water, unable to escape from it. The insect has been caught in the surface-binding force.

This force also accounts for the way water and other liquids form drops or droplets, for example on a kitchen table after some liquid has been spilled. The liquid molecules bind to one another more strongly than they bind to the molecules of the table top, and so they round up into droplets.

Sometimes, though, liquid molecules will bind even more strongly to other surfaces than to each other. This happens to water in an upright glass tube. The surface water molecules are attracted more to the glass than to each other, so that the top of the water curves up towards the sides of the tube.

Water
Water is the most important liquid in our lives. Our bodies are made mostly of water, and all forms of life on Earth soon die if they have to go without it. The diagram shows another important aspect of water – how it moves around the face of the Earth and helps to make the weather.

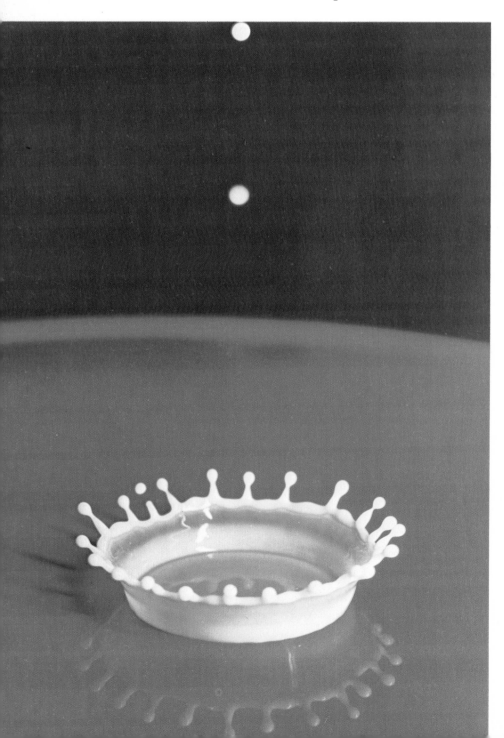

◄ Caught in a high speed camera shot, a drop of milk hits and splashes up from the ground. The liquid drops breaking away from the almost perfectly symmetrical shape are themselves nearly perfect spheres. This ball shape is caused by the attraction of surface molecules for one another, and is the shape that uses up least energy.

◄ Water curves upwards around the stick. This results from the water molecules binding more strongly to the stick than to each other.

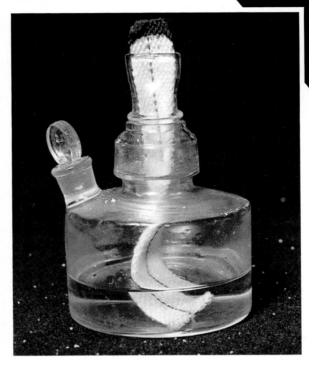

◄ In this lamp, liquid creeps up the wick from bottom to top. This upward creeping movement is called capillary action.

▼ Water is vital to life. The picture shows how water and moisture move around in the natural world.

The water cycle

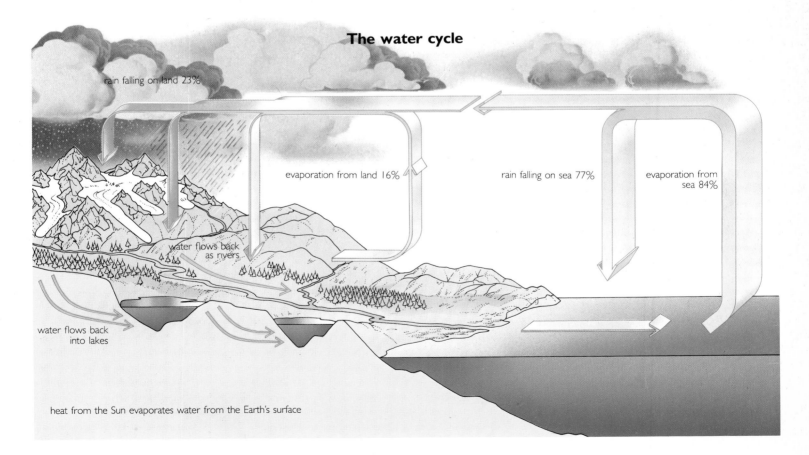

rain falling on land 23%

evaporation from land 16%

rain falling on sea 77%

evaporation from sea 84%

water flows back as rivers

water flows back into lakes

heat from the Sun evaporates water from the Earth's surface

towards the surface and escape into the air. This can go on happening until there is no water left at all (*not* good for the pan if the heat is still on). All the water has turned into steam, which has then cooled in the air to make a cloud of tiny droplets, or water vapour – just like the clouds in the sky.

Freezing

If, instead of heating or evaporating water, you chill or freeze it, as in a refrigerator, the water turns into ice, or solid water.

Other liquids can be frozen too, though some, such as alcohol, do not freeze or go solid until very low temperatures are reached. For this reason polar explorers took thermometers filled with alcohol with them on their journeys. Even at the South or North Poles the alcohol stayed unfrozen in the thermometer and so continued to show the correct temperature.

Melting

If the refrigerator is switched off all the ice in the icebox melts. The water there has warmed up to become liquid again, with messy results.

▲ When a liquid is heated enough, it will boil to become a gas. A piece of plastic film on the top of this boiling water is being lifted by the steam escaping from the water. Crystals have been placed in the water to show how the water molecules move around faster, as the water is heated.

The water cycle diagram on page 13 shows how clouds are formed from water molecules evaporated off the sea by the heat of the Sun. This happens because the Sun's heat gives the water molecules more energy, so that they move around faster and finally escape from the sea's surface to become a vapour or cloud. Another example of evaporation is wet clothes drying on a line hung outside. In this case, the wind helps to carry water molecules away from the clothes, until these become dry.

If any liquid is warmed, heated or wind-blown enough, it will turn entirely into a vapour or a gas. When a pan of water boils, the bubbles of steam rush

▶ The space rocket's engine contains two liquid gases, that is, gases that have been made liquid at very low temperatures. One of the liquid gases is oxygen, the other is the rocket fuel. When these liquids are allowed to become gases again, and mixed together, they burst into the roaring flame of the rocket engine. The gases also take up much more space than the liquids, so that they push the rocket upwards.

WHAT ARE SOLIDS?

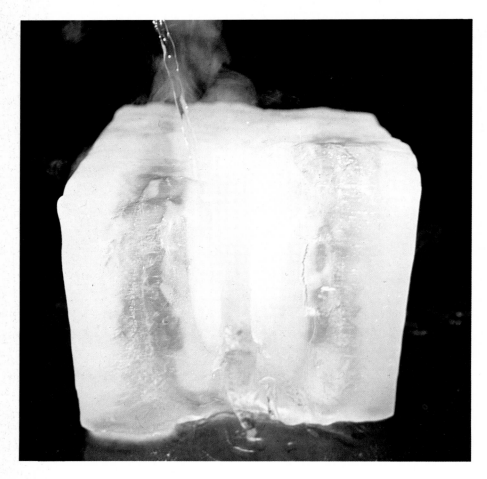

▲ Some boiling water is being poured onto a block of ice or solid water. This causes the ice to melt into liquid water. Although it may seem very unlikely, this melted water stays at ice temperature, 0°C (32°F), until the whole mass has melted, after which more boiling water will raise the temperature.

We know that a chair is a solid object because it feels hard. But what about rubber and butter? They are solids too, but can be soft. And if you have ever 'belly-flopped' while diving into a swimming pool, you will know that even liquid water can feel very hard! So, what exactly *is* a solid?

For an answer to this question we must return to molecules. First, remember that a molecule of any substance is either a single one of its atoms, or two or more of its atoms stuck together. Next, remember that the molecules of a gas are far apart from one another, so do not attract one another much, and therefore fly about freely. The molecules of a liquid are closer together, so attract one another enough for the liquid to stay more or less together, although it will flow about if it gets the chance.

In a solid, molecules are very close and attract one another so much that the solid always stays together in one place. But a rubbery or buttery solid will easily change its shape, if pushed or pulled.

Crystals and non-crystals
The hardest solids are *crystals* such as gemstones – if you have a ring with a ruby or other bright stone, you will know just how hard and sharp this feels. Ordinary sugar also consists of crystals, but these are less hard and sharp. In all kinds of crystals, atoms or molecules are bound together in a definite pattern. In a ruby, they are bound extremely hard in one pattern, and in the sugar crystal they are bound not quite so hard in another pattern. The different patterns make up the different crystal shapes.

But not all solids are made up of crystals. Instead their atoms or molecules are bound together strongly enough to make a solid, but not in any definite crystal shape or pattern. Soft, buttery or rubbery solids are of this kind.

But matter is full of surprises, and some of the solids not made up of crystals can feel very hard. Ordinary window glass certainly feels hard, yet it is not, like the transparent ruby, a hard, crystalline solid. In fact, the glass is flowing very, very slowly – it is really a very hard liquid!

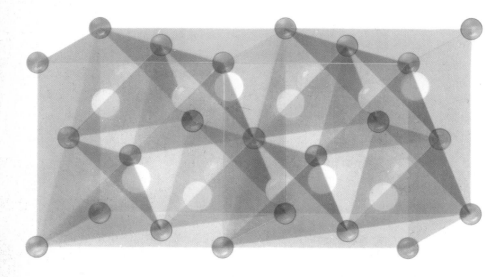

◀ Atoms in an alloy or mixture of the metal zinc (pink) and the non-metal selenium (blue). These atoms are linked strongly to one another in the regular shape of crystals.

16

► Crystals are the hardest and most regularly-shaped forms of solid matter. The pictures show large mineral crystals, both types of which are shaped like long prisms. The mineral **right** is pyromorphite, that **below** is wavellite.

HEAVIEST AND LIGHTEST

Which is heavier, a ton of feathers or a ton of coal? A ton of feathers weighs just the same as a ton of anything else, yet we think of feathers as light. What we really mean is that a feather is lightweight for its size. A piece of gold in the shape of a feather would be much heavier. When scientists talk about how heavy or light a substance is for its size, they talk about its density. In this book, when we talk about something being very heavy we mean it is very heavy for its size – or very dense.

You may have seen a hydrogen-filled balloon float through the air, which is a much heavier gas than the hydrogen that fills the balloon. (Remember that hydrogen is the lightest of substances.)

Liquids are heavier than gases. So are solids heavier than liquids? Not always. Many solids are lighter – think of the way wood and bottle corks float.

Heavy metals

Metals include the heaviest substances known here on Earth. Most metals, including the very heavy ones, are solids at ordinary temperatures. Like those other solids, sugar and the ruby, metals are made up of crystals. But usually, metal crystals can only be seen through a microscope.

The heavy metal mercury is unusual because it is a liquid at ordinary room temperatures. If you look at a thermometer you will see a silvery column of this liquid metal. The liquid mercury is heavier, or denser, than the hard glass of the thermometer.

The metal gold is heavier even than mercury. The heaviest substance on Earth is the metal osmium. Even rarer than gold, osmium is $22\frac{1}{2}$ times as heavy as water.

Super-heavy substances

Osmium may be very heavy, but in the Universe are substances that make even osmium seem 'light as a feather'. These super-heavy substances are special sorts of star.

One kind of super-heavy star is called a white dwarf. This is a small star whose atoms have become packed down very closely, so that a piece of white dwarf has many, many more atoms than a piece of Earth matter of the same size. For this reason it is much heavier than Earth substances.

▼ Platinum jewelry is even more of a status symbol than gold, because platinum is both rarer and more expensive. It is also heavier, being one of the densest of all metals.

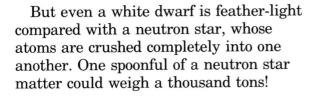

In some situation[s] bodies seem to lo[se] their weight. The scuba diver **left** c[an] swim around wit[h] hardly any effort despite his heavy [?]. This contains compressed air, w[hich] gives him extra buoyancy, or lift, [?] water. The astro[naut] (**below**) weighs nothing at all. H[is] body floats at zer[o] gravity inside his [?].

But even a white dwarf is feather-light compared with a neutron star, whose atoms are crushed completely into one another. One spoonful of a neutron star matter could weigh a thousand tons!

▲ Why does the sky look red? This happens at morning and evening, when the Sun is low down and its rays have to travel farthest through the Earth's atmosphere – which filters out all but the red rays that reach our eyes.

So far we have established that even a hard, solid object such as a chair is made up of invisible atoms and molecules far too small to see. The same applies to liquids such as water and gases such as air. Our own bodies, being made up of a mixture of solids, liquids and gases, are also made up of invisible atoms and molecules, and so are the bodies of all other living creatures and plants. If this is so, is there anything else in the world, or in the whole Universe, that is *not* made up of atoms and molecules?

Smaller than atoms
For a quick answer to that question, look at the diagram on page 6. This shows atoms of solids, liquids, gases and plasmas. A plasma is a gas that has been heated to such a high temperature that its atoms have begun to break down into smaller parts, known as *sub-atomic particles*. They are called sub-atomic because they are even smaller than atoms, and particles because although they are so very, very small, they do have some weight and so can still be called

particles of matter. Sub-atomic particles include such things as electrons that flow as electricity in the wires of your house, radio or TV. So as well as atoms and molecules, the Universe contains lots and lots of sub-atomic particles such as electrons.

Glowing matter
A star is a great ball of gas. It is at such a very high temperature that the gas is really a plasma that gives off electrons and other sub-atomic particles. These are quite invisible to us, but we know that the nearest of all stars, our own Sun, also gives off light that we can see and heat that we can feel. The Sun is not the only matter to do this. The other stars and all other kinds of matter – for example, a piece of metal – will glow with light and give off heat if heated up enough.

▶ Why does the sky look blue? The answer is, because of the way light rays from the Sun are scattered by air. Sunlight is made up of all colours, but its blue waves or rays are the most scattered, so making the sky look blue, as over this South American volcano.

Light and heat are different from sub-atomic particles such as electrons. They are weightless, so are not regarded as matter. Light and heat are examples of *energy* which moves in waves or rays between one lump of matter and the next – between a star and the Earth, or between the heated metal and our bodies. So the Universe, besides containing lots of matter, also contains lots of energy.

Waves and rays

Another good example of matter and its energy is the water wave you make in the bath, or see coming in at the seaside. The water, of course, is liquid matter which is moving in one direction or another – along the bath, or towards the shore. But each wave really only moves up and down, as the water travels along. You can see this by floating a cork on the

bathwater. This will move mostly up-and-down as the water waves pass by it. And the bigger the wave the more energy the waves have, the more the cork will bob up and down.

Light and heat, too, travel in waves, but these are not waves of matter such as water waves. They are waves of pure energy, travelling between one lump of matter and the next. Heat and light waves are very much smaller than water waves. Their vibrations, that is up-and-down or back-and-forth movements, are so small that they are barely a squiggle, so that the path of heat or light energy is

▼ Earth is continuously bombarded with rays from outer space. These cosmic rays begin to spiral round and round when they enter the Earth's magnetism. The curved lines are those of the Earth's magnetic field of force.

▲ Molecules of air (white circles) scatter blue light rays more than yellow or red light rays.

22

almost a straight line. Scientists call this nearly-straight squiggle a *ray* of energy, so that it doesn't matter whether you say light wave or light ray because it means the same thing. (But a heat wave, of course, means hot weather!)

Travelling energy

Pure energy waves, such as those of heat and light, are very different from matter waves such as water waves, because the more energy they contain, the *smaller* their up-and-down or back-and-forth movements. But there are some other kinds of energy waves that travel in smaller or tighter squiggles still, so have even more energy. X-rays, for example, have such a tight squiggle and so much energy that they can pass right through many solid objects. Since they will pass through flesh but not bone, they are used to make accurate pictures of the insides of our bodies. Doctors find these very useful, for example in discovering where and how a bone is broken.

Radioactivity

In a hospital X-ray machine, metal atoms are made to give off X-rays by being bombarded, or hit hard, with electrons. But atoms of some metals and other substances also give off penetrating rays quite naturally, without any such bombardment. These substances are called radioactive. They are quite common, for example in the Earth's rocks. Radioactivity means that their atoms are breaking down naturally to give off various kinds of waves, rays and particles.

▲ X-rays can penetrate through cloth and flesh, but not so easily through bone. When the penetrating X-rays hit a photographic plate they make a picture like this.

◄ Radioactive substances can be very dangerous because the rays and particles they give off can damage our bodies. In the lab, they are handled remotely like this. The protective window contains lead metal atoms, which absorb all radioactivity so that it cannot harm the handler.

▼ Electrical energy in New York at night. The electricity for all the lights comes mostly from power stations that burn oil or coal, rather in the way that the diesel loco burns oil to make electrical energy.

WHAT IS ENERGY?

On Earth, the most familiar kinds of travelling energy are the light waves that allow us to see things, and the heat rays that help keep us warm.

Other useful kinds of travelling energy are radio and TV waves, which travel through air and space to bring us programmes in sound and pictures. Both of these are the same kind of energy as heat and light waves, except that their waves are longer and not like squiggles. In contrast, some kinds of travelling energy, such as X-rays, travel in much shorter and more squiggly waves or rays.

X-rays are very penetrating rays. In hospitals, they are made in special machines and are used to make X-ray pictures and to treat illnesses such as cancer. Because they are so penetrating, such rays can also be harmful. Outside our own Earth, the stars send off huge amounts of penetrating rays, and lots of these reach the Earth, particularly from the nearest star, our own Sun. If these rays reached our bodies they would damage them, but the Earth's protective blanket of air soaks up most of these harmful rays before they reach us. Though if you have ever got badly sunburned, you will know that even the rays that do reach us can be harmful!

Non-travelling, or locked-up, energy
Besides the various kinds of travelling energy – the rays and waves – we have looked at so far, there are many other kinds of energy that do not travel freely about but are locked-up. These kinds of energy may be locked up in the stars, until they turn into travelling forms of energy such as light, heat and X-rays.

Down here on Earth, energy is locked-up in natural substances, coal and oil, for example. In the last two hundred years or so, human beings have become much more expert in unlocking Nature's energy. This is what we call modern technology. Radio and TV waves are examples of energy unlocked by man – but there are many other examples, as we will see.

▲ A fuel such as coal contains stored chemical energy. When coal burns, some of this energy is released as heat. The carbon (C) in the coal joins with the oxygen (O=O) in the air to make the gas carbon dioxide (O=C=O), plus heat and flames.

▼ When water is hot enough, it will boil to make steam. But there has been no chemical change in the water as there is in coal (**above**). Liquid water has the same group of atoms (H–O–H) as steam.

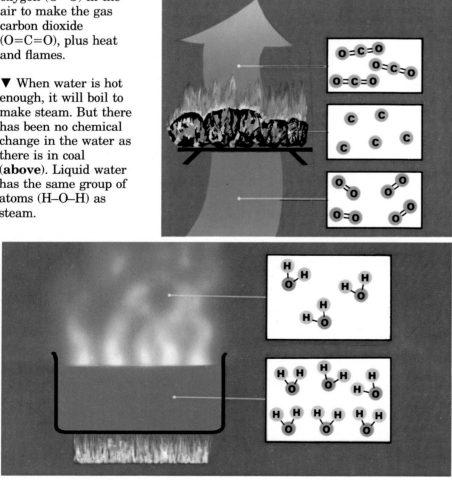

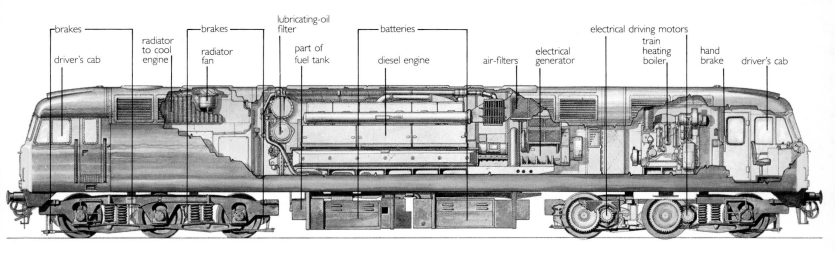

brakes

driver's cab

radiator to cool engine

brakes

radiator fan

lubricating-oil filter

part of fuel tank

batteries

diesel engine

air-filters

electrical generator

electrical driving motors

train heating boiler

hand brake

driver's cab

▲ This big locomotive uses both stored chemical energy and electrical energy. The stored chemical energy is in its diesel oil fuel. This is burned in its diesel engine, which turns the loco's electrical generator, which makes electricity. The electricity operates the loco's electrical driving motors, which drive the wheels.

▼ This giant mirror is called a solar furnace. It reflects the Sun's rays so that they concentrate or focus at a point in the tower building. The focussed rays can be used to melt metals or heat water to make steam to be used for making electricity.

ENERGY AND FORCE

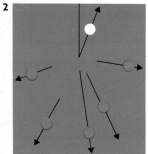

▲ **1** In the game of snooker, a white ball is knocked towards coloured balls. The white ball has movement-energy.
2 When it hits the red balls it forces them away so that they now have movement-energy too.

Stored energy

Something can have a lot of energy just because it is high up. If you climb up a ladder with a football and put this on a ledge or in a fork of a tree the football just rests quietly – so where is all its energy? If the football is knocked from its settled position, down it goes, to bounce energetically off the ground. The height of the bounce shows the amount of its energy.

Another thing to notice about this experiment is that it needs energy to climb up the ladder and put the football on its perch, and that the higher the perch, the more energy is needed to climb there. All this energy was somehow used up when the ball toppled down, because after a bounce or two, it comes to rest again. So, while it was perched up there, the ball was somehow storing its energy.

Energy can be stored in other ways too. A bomb, for instance, before it goes off, stores an awful lot of energy. In a less dangerous way, a lump of sugar or a piece of cake stores energy. You know that when you feel very hungry, a good meal gives you the energy to keep going.

Force

Suppose that in the football experiment, your head is directly under the ball. You feel the force of the football as it bounces off your head. So the energy of a moving ball or other object can be experienced as a force.

In the case of a bomb going off, our bodies feel the much greater force of the explosion. The energy that was locked up in the bomb has been released, with very forceful effects. Inside the engine cylinders of a truck or automobile, explosions happen when the gasoline or

◄ Power stations of today, which supply our homes and factories with electricity, use huge electrical generators such as this one.

▲ The sound reflectors on the ceiling of the concert hall make sure that everyone in the audience can hear everything that the orchestra is playing. Sound energy travels as waves of air, which bounce off the reflectors to reach the ears of the audience (**left**).

diesel fuel is ignited or set alight by the engine spark. In this case, when energy is released from the exploding fuel, it provides the force that starts up the engine and keeps it going, and moves the vehicle along.

Electricity can also provide the force to make an engine or motor go. Some electric trains take their electricity from the rails or wires in which it is stored. The vacuum cleaner and refrigerator in your home both have small electric motors, which take their electricity from the house wiring.

▲ Tokyo, like other great modern cities, is a hive of energy. Extra-energetic is the high-speed train in the foreground.

ATOMS AND THE UNIVERSE

▶ The atom's electrons (green) are held whizzing around its nucleus by a short-distance electrical force.

▼ The planet Saturn's moons (green) are held in orbit around it by the long-distance force of gravity. Saturn's rings (**bottom**) are particles of ice held in orbit by the force of gravity.

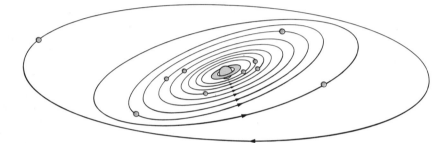

From smallest to largest, everything in the Universe is ruled by invisible forces. First, let us look at some of the very smallest things – atoms. As you know, atoms are the smallest bits of matter from which each different kind of substance is made up.

But as we discovered on page 20, each different kind of atom is made up of still smaller parts, the sub-atomic particles. Every kind of atom contains at least one of the sub-atomic particles called electrons. These electrons whirl around the nucleus, the central part of the atom.

As the electrons whirl, they obviously have plenty of energy. So why, you may ask, don't they leave the atom and whirl off somewhere else? The answer is that the electrons are held inside the atom by a force of attraction. This is an electrical force. In fact, it is the same electrical force that drives the motor in your kitchen refrigerator or vacuum cleaner.

Now, an atom is nothing like a vacuum cleaner, so how does electrical force hold

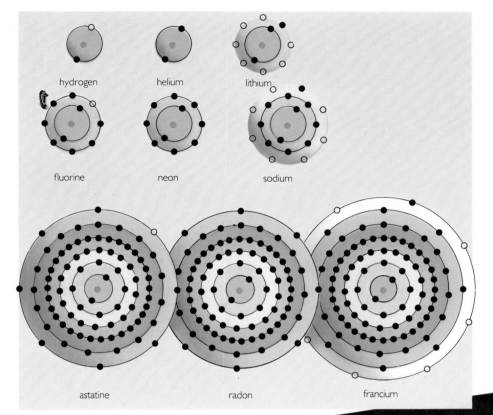

hydrogen   helium   lithium

fluorine   neon   sodium

astatine   radon   francium

◄ Atoms come in various sizes. The simplest and smallest atom is that of the gas hydrogen. The metal francium, for example, has a much larger, more complicated atom.

▼ Right across the Universe, stars and other forms of matter are affected by the force of gravity. These galaxies, each containing thousands of millions of stars, are held in their spiral shape by gravity. Each galaxy, too, affects every other galaxy by the force of gravity, no matter how vast the distances.

the electrons inside it? The answer to this question is something called electrical charge, which can be positive or negative. Positive and negative electrical charges attract, or pull at one another. In atoms, the electrons have a negative charge and the nucleus has a positive charge, and the pull or attraction between them keeps the electrons in their proper places as they whirl around the nucleus.

Long-distance force

The way that an electron travels around the nucleus in an atom, is rather similar to the way the Earth travels around the Sun during the year, or the way the Moon travels around the Earth each month. Although, of course, the atom is on a tiny scale, compared to the Sun, Earth and Moon.

There is another difference too. Whereas the electron is held in its path around the nucleus by a force of electrical attraction, the Earth is held in its path around the Sun, and the Moon in its path around the Earth, by a much longer-distance force called gravity. This force is so long-distance that it pulls even on the remotest stars at the far ends of the Universe.

THE STRONGEST FORCES

Electrons are held inside their atoms by electrical force, but scientists can easily pull electrons away from their atoms because the electrical force is not very strong. Gravity is a weaker force still. It is the long-distance force that pulls on all forms of matter, from stars and planets right down to the football that fell down to Earth on page 26. In the case of the football, it was one piece of matter, and the Earth was the other, and they pulled one another by the force of gravity, which is why the football fell down. Although gravity acts over such long distances it is the weakest of forces. You know how easy it is, here on Earth, to pick up a ball and so overcome the force of gravity.

Nuclear force

If electrical force is not very strong, and the force of gravity is weak, then what are the strongest forces? One answer is given by the picture of the H-bomb. This super-destructive bomb is called a nuclear weapon, because its explosion results from the breakup of the nucleus, or central part, of many, many atoms. The result, as you can see, is a tremendous release of force and energy. So the force that held each nucleus together before the explosion must also have been extremely strong. Nuclear force, in fact, is the strongest short-distance force in the Universe.

Matter into energy

When many atoms break up, as they do in the H-bomb and other nuclear weapons, what happens to the pieces? The answer is, that the pieces either form smaller kinds of atoms, or else stick together to make fewer larger atoms. In either case, some matter is always 'left over' and does not go towards making the new kinds of atoms. This left-over matter is what turns into energy, to make the huge explosion of the H-bomb or atomic bomb. In such a bomb, even a tiny bit of matter will turn into an enormous amount of energy.

This also explains how the stars burn or shine. Like a giant, slow, H-bomb, a star gets all its energy from the breaking-up and sticking-together of its atoms. The 'left-over' matter of these atoms turns into vast amounts of light, heat and other kinds of wave and ray energy. This energy travels out through space, for example, as the heat and light we receive from our nearest star, the Sun.

► Matter and antimatter are opposites and annihilate one another if they ever come into contact. Far out in space, this may account for some of the super-energetic explosions that astronomers sometimes observe. The matter would consist mostly of atoms of hydrogen gas. The antimatter would consist mostly of atoms of anti-hydrogen gas. When they come into contact, these atoms destroy one another with the production of radiant energy.

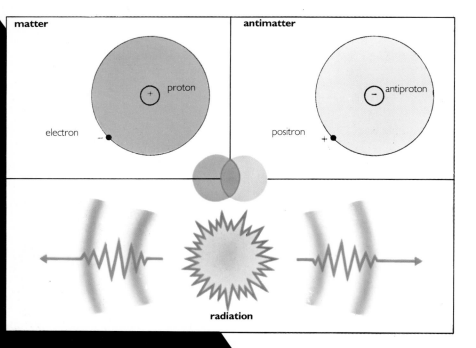

► An H-bomb explosion, the most destructive force yet released by man. This force is the one that holds the nucleus of the atom together. It is also the force that makes the stars shine. In nuclear weapons such as the H-bomb, the force is released suddenly and destructively. By contrast, the stars release their nuclear force slowly and steadily.

30

OTHER STRONG FORCES

Earth forces
When scientists first made an atomic bomb, near the end of World War 2, (1939–45), they released hidden forces of tremendous destructive power. And later H-bombs were thousands of times more powerful and destructive than the first atomic bomb. Yet the Earth, left entirely to itself, produces from time to time explosions that make even the H-bomb look small.

For example, in 1883 a South Sea island named Krakatoa blew up with such force that the explosion was heard 4,800 km (3,000 miles) away. Waves produced by the force of the explosion travelled for as much as 11,000 km (7,000 miles), swamping many coasts and islands as they did so, and drowning many thousands of people.

Krakatoa was a particularly violent example of a volcanic eruption. Volcanoes erupt when hot gases and steam build up to form great pressure underground in the Earth's crust, then suddenly break through, sometimes with explosive power.

The heat and pressure for a volcanic eruption come from deeper down, under the crust, where the Earth is generally much hotter and more violent than on its surface.

Magnetism
Magnetism is a quite different Earth force. This force extends all around the Earth and as far out into space as 16,000 km (10,000 miles). Down here on Earth you can easily detect, or find out, the direction of the Earth's magnetic force, with a simple magnetic compass. The force acts on the metal needle of the compass, making it always point north.

The Earth is a giant magnet, but you will also know of much smaller magnets, the ones made from iron that can be used to attract pins and other small iron or steel objects. Iron and iron *alloys* show the strongest magnetism of all substances.

Cousin forces
Very strong magnets, or *electro-magnets*, are made by wrapping an iron bar with many turns of specially-coated wire, then passing an electric current through the wire. Because electric force and magnetic force are 'cousins' this will make the electro-magnet so strong that it will attract and pick up quite heavy metal objects, for example, automobiles are picked up in this way in scrap yards.

▼ Magnetic force shows up most clearly when some iron filings are placed around a metal magnet. The filings are formed into this pattern by the magnetic force field.

▲ Electrons can have a lot of energy. This beam of electrons has partly melted the steel tube (bottom).

32

▲ Erupting volcanoes such as Mount Etna in Sicily reveal the vast energy of the Earth's hot interior. In the large picture, lava or red-hot liquid rock is flowing down a slope of the volcano. An eruption from the summit (**inset**) flings red-hot rock and cinders high in the air.

◄ Hot water geysers, such as this one in Iceland, are also proof of the heat energy in the Earth's crust.

CHEMICAL FORCES

If you leave a bicycle out in the rain, its wheels and handlebars will soon go rusty. If you light a candle and let it burn, eventually it will all be used up. If you leave a loaf of bread uncovered for a day or two, it gets so hard that you can hardly cut it.

These three changes all have something in common. Guessed it? Well, all the changes happened in the air. The bicycle's steel parts changed in wet air – to go rusty. The bread also changed in air, to become very hard on its outside. The candle changed too, although this time it took a lighted match to make it do so, and it then burned more or less cheerfully – in air.

In fact, what all these changes needed was the oxygen in the air. The steel parts of the bicycle combined with the oxygen to make rust. The bread combined with the oxygen to make harder bread. The candle combined with the oxygen to make gas and soot. These combinations with oxygen are called oxidation, which is an extremely common type of chemical change.

Changing substances

How can you tell chemical changes from other kinds of change in the world around you? For example, if water spills out of a glass, is this a chemical change? No, because the water itself is still there, either in the glass or spilled on the table or floor. Suppose, however, you heat the water in a pan or kettle until it turns into steam. Is this a chemical change? No, because the steam, although it looks different from the water in the glass, is really still the same substance.

The same would apply if you heated a bit of solid metal until it melted to become a liquid. This would still not be a chemical change – *unless* as you were heating the metal, some or all of it combined with oxygen or nitrogen, the main gases in the air.

If this happened, the substance, when it cooled again to become a solid, would not only look different but would also be made up differently, because it would be a combination of metal and nitrogen or oxygen. Chemical changes, therefore, are changes of substance.

▶ When the gas acetylene is burned in oxygen its flame is so hot that it can be used to cut thick metal, or, as in the picture, to weld metal pipes together.

◄ Two miners at work in the Italian Alps. The miner with his back to the camera is drilling a hole in which explosives, probably dynamite, will be placed. The explosives will be detonated (set off) by remote control to bring down the rock.

▼ An explosive such as dynamite stores a tremendous amount of chemical energy, as this quarry explosion shows.

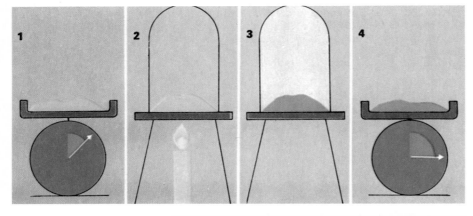

▲ Oxidation – one kind of chemical change.
1 A substance is weighed.
2 It is burned in a bell jar.
3 Oxygen is taken from the air.
4 The oxidized substance weighs more.

► Strong acids are very active chemical compounds. They will, for example, quickly dissolve many metals.

▼ Vinegar is an acid substance that will partly dissolve bone, to make it soft enough to tie in knots.

▲ Strong acids are made in large chemical factories, such as nitric acid plants. If strong nitric acid gets on the skin, it causes an orange-brown burn.

Chemical substances

In a way, all substances are chemical substances, from very complicated ones like the substances of our bodies, down to very simple ones such as the salt we put on our food. The substances of living bodies contain many different kinds of atoms, linked together in many complicated ways. Common household salt has only two kinds of atom: those of a metal called sodium and a gas called chlorine.

Notice that common salt looks nothing like either a metal or a gas – this is another example of substances combining together to make something quite different – a typical chemical change. Sodium and chlorine themselves are, of course, even simpler substances than common salt. Does anything combine together chemically to make sodium or chlorine?

No, because sodium and chlorine are examples of the simplest kinds of chemical substances which contain only one kind of atom. The metal sodium contains only atoms of sodium, and the gas chlorine contains only atoms of chlorine.

These, and the other simplest chemical substances, are called *chemical elements*. (You may know the word elementary, meaning easy or simple.) Iron and oxygen, which combine to form rust (page 34) are two other chemical elements. Altogether there are 92 different chemical elements in Nature, which combine chemically to form all the substances and materials of the world, simple and complicated, common and rare.

Chemical compounds

Chemical elements, the simplest kinds of substance, combine together to make more complicated substances called *chemical compounds*. Common salt and rust are only two of the millions of chemical compounds there are.

Some chemical compounds are more reactive or forceful than others. Common salt is more reactive than rust, that is, it will cause further chemical changes to happen more easily. A strong acid such as nitric acid is a chemical compound even more reactive than common salt.

Simple and complicated molecules

To say that a chemical compound is simple or complicated, is the same as saying that its molecule is little or big. A molecule of a chemical compound is two or more different kinds of atoms linked or bonded together. The simple compound common salt has a molecule of one sodium atom bonded with one chlorine atom. Equally simple is the molecule of the strong acid called hydrochloric acid, which has one hydrogen atom bonded with one chlorine atom. We can write this more simply still as HCl, using the letter H for hydrogen and the letters Cl for chlorine.

So far we have looked at only very simple chemical compounds, with small molecules. More complicated molecules have more atoms, often of more than two kinds. Ordinary sugar, for example, has atoms of three kinds – carbon or C, hydrogen or H, and oxygen or O. Each molecule has twelve C's, twenty-two H's and eleven O's so that it contains 45 atoms altogether.

Even though this is a bit more complicated, sugars are among the simplest of the chemical compounds that make up the bodies of animals, plants and other living creatures. Most of the chemical compounds which form living organisms have hundreds, thousands, or even hundreds of thousands, of atoms in their molecules. Although these molecules of life can be so complicated, they mostly contain only six different kinds of chemical element out of the 92 that there are altogether. These six elements of life are C, H and O (as in sugar) together with N or nitrogen, P or phosphorus and S or sulphur.

Marvellous metal molecules

Most molecules of life chemicals have only these six kinds of atom, but two of them in particular, each absolutely vital to life, also have a metal atom in their molecules. The first of these compounds is chlorophyll, the green substance in leaves and other parts of living plants. Chlorophyll, which enables plants to build up their bodies from the carbon dioxide of the air, has an atom of the metal magnesium, or Mg, in the middle of its

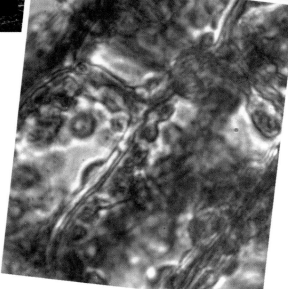

very complicated molecule.

The second of the marvellous metal molecules is hemoglobin. This is the molecule that carries vital oxygen in blood cells, to nourish the living tissues of our bodies. In this case the metal atom is iron or Fe. (Fe is short for *ferrum*, the Latin word for iron.)

▲ Trees, like other forms of life, grow by chemical processes. Most of a tree's great bulk is made up of chemical compounds of carbon. The tree gets its carbon from the air.

◄ In this picture, a bit of tree leaf is magnified more than 1,000 times. The green blobs inside the cells are *chloroplasts*, which contain the green chemical substance called chlorophyll. This is what turns the carbon dioxide of the air into the carbon compounds that build up the body of the tree. The building-up process also needs energy from sunlight, and moisture.

▼ Peat is the remains of plants that died and became buried many thousands of years ago. Its chemical energy is released by burning, so that it is useful as a fuel. This peat cutter lives in Ireland.

ENERGY FOR LIFE

What is food?

You know that automobiles need gasoline or petrol to make them go. The gasoline is a fuel that stores chemical energy. When it is burned in the engine's cylinders, its energy is released, providing the force to turn the automobile's wheels.

Food is the fuel our bodies need to make them go, because it, too, stores chemical energy. When food is burned in our bodies, it releases its energy for all our various activities – running, jumping, or just breathing in and out.

You may not think of breathing as an activity, but it is, in fact, very important because we need oxygen from the air for the burning, or oxidation, of our food, to provide us with energy.

Quick energy and slow energy

Not all of our food is burned up immediately to provide us with energy for running, jumping, etc. We also need food to build up our bodies, particularly when we are young and still growing fast. Even when we are fully grown, parts of our bodies always need repair. Each day, thousands of body cells die and must be replaced. So we need food for growth and repair as well as for muscle-energy.

▲ The butterfly stroke takes a lot of energy!

Some foods, such as sugar, provide quick energy. They are quickly burned up in the body. Athletes often take swigs of glucose or sugar drink to provide themselves with quick energy. But if you eat too many sweets or too much candy and don't take enough exercise you don't feel more energetic – you get fat! When your body has had enough sugar for its needs, it stops burning up the sugar, and instead turns it into fat.

Being too fat isn't good for your health, but your body does need a certain amount of fat. For one thing, fat is a good 'inner overcoat' for keeping the body warm. More important still, fat is a provider of slow energy. The body burns it more slowly than sugar, and so it acts as an energy store. Your body needs this slow energy as much as the fast muscle-energy. Inside your body, thousands of chemical reactions are going on at the same time, and most of them need some energy. Even digesting your food, the energy provider itself, needs energy!

▲ Body energy also appears as muscle power, such as that shown by these high-leaping dolphins.

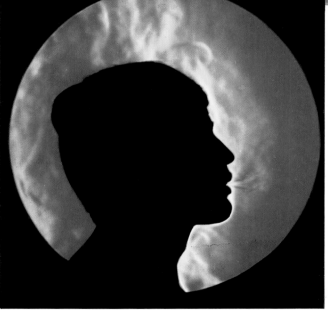

► Some of the energy we get from our food leaves our bodies as heat. The picture shows swirls of heated air.

▼ Sugary foods give us quick energy. A lump of sugar will burn to release its energy. After the burning, all that is left is a little sooty carbon.

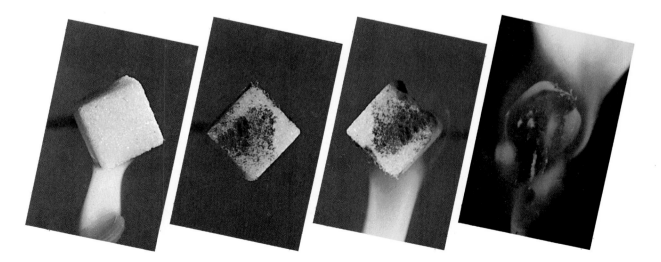

VITAL BODY CHEMICALS

If you have ever licked a cut from which blood is oozing, you will have noticed that your blood tasts salty. This is not surprising because blood contains quite a lot of common salt or sodium chloride (page 36).

But the chemistry of living bodies is really very complicated, and most body chemicals have far bigger and more complicated molecules than that of common salt with its two atoms. Some of these complicated body chemicals are mainly concerned with energy, for example sugar and fat.

Body-building chemicals

Chemicals for energy are extremely important, but our bodies need chemicals for growth as well. Our food provides many body-building, or growth, chemicals. Can you name some of the substances that help to build up your body? If some people are very fat, their bodies are obviously mainly built up of fatty chemicals. Most people, though, would rather have a muscly body than a fat one. Muscle is built chiefly of chemicals called proteins, that have huge molecules even more complicated than most fat or sugar molecules. Protein molecules are built up in our bodies from many smaller chemical molecules called amino-acids.

Animal bodies such as our own are mostly built up, if they are healthy, of muscle and bone. These are tough, strong tissues which act as the inner framework of the body, holding everything else in place and allowing movements such as standing and walking.

Living plants also need to stand up in the air to catch sunlight, and need to resist the power of the wind to blow them

▲ In very small quantities, vitamins are essential for our health. This is a crystal of the Vitamin B$_1$ magnified many hundreds of times. B$_1$ is in lean meat, poultry, fish, whole-grain bread and cereals. People whose diet lacks Vitamin B$_1$ develop a disease called beriberi.

► Grapefruit and oranges are rich in Vitamin C

Sweet potatoes and potatoes are rich in starch and sugar

Cabbage provides us with fibre

Avocadoes provide oil

Apples are good for slimmers!

Liver is rich in Vitamin B$_2$

Milk and spinach are very good for you!

Beef is rich in muscle-building proteins

Eggs are a whole food – rich in many food substances

Bread gives us starch

Yeast tablets are rich in Vitamin B$_2$

Cheese, like milk, is rich in proteins and fats

grapefruit   oranges   strawberries   sweet potatoes   potatoe

40

◄ The colourful floating market in Curaçao, an island in the West Indies. Instead of the usual market stalls, boats are piled high with the produce that is for sale and tied up at quays beside the street.

raw cabbage   avocadoes   apples   liver   pasteurised milk   spinach   beef   eggs   white bread   yeast tablets   cheese

down. Their strong, tough framework is woody. Wood is built up of chemicals called cellulose and lignin. These also have giant, complicated molecules. But the molecules of cellulose and lignin, unlike those of proteins, are built up of many sugar-like molecules linked together.

Enzymes

Living plants, as well as animals, have many proteins in their bodies, although these are not muscle-forming proteins. Many plant and animal proteins of the non-muscly sort are known as *enzymes*. These are among the most vital of all the chemicals of life, because without them most of the body's chemical reactions could not take place. In other words, life would stop dead without enzymes.

The biggest molecules of all

Of all the chemical molecules we have looked at so far in this book, proteins are the biggest. Many proteins in the bodies of animals, plants and other living organisms are truly giant molecules, containing up to hundreds of thousands of atoms.

Just as large, or sometimes even larger, are the molecules of another kind of

◄ The giant redwood needs a particularly tough, strong chemical framework to support its huge bulk.

▼ Wild polar bears get the body chemicals they need from the seals and other animals they feed on.

chemical compound found in all living organisms. These compounds are called the nucleic acids. They are found mostly inside the nucleus of the living cell. (Science can be confusing – the cell nucleus has nothing to do with the atomic nucleus described earlier in the book. But in both cases, the word 'nucleus' means 'central part'.)

Proteins, as we have seen, play very important parts in living bodies. Not only do they make up the muscle of animal bodies, but the proteins known as enzymes are vital to all forms of life, to make their chemical reactions go on working.

Giant nucleic acids are equally vital to all forms of life. It is the nucleic acids that cause enzymes and other proteins to be made in living cells. So the nucleic acids are really the chemical masters or brains behind all living processes.

Molecules of heredity
The nucleic acid known as DNA is one of the most important of these substances because it controls the way we inherit our features and other characteristics from our parents. Another way of saying this is that DNA is the molecule of heredity, or inheritance.

Every person's or creature's DNA is unique. That is, it is slightly different from the DNA of even the closest relative. This is because DNA, being a huge molecule with an enormous number of atoms, can have them arranged in a

tremendous number of different ways. The DNA in each living cell in your body is your very own type, with its own special arrangement of atoms – no one else will have an arrangement like it, unless you are one of a pair of identical twins. This uniqueness is due to the fact that the egg from which you developed contained DNA from both your father and your mother. And since your DNA is the cause of all your special features, this explains why you may have, say, 'your mother's eyes and your father's ears' but at the same time be completely yourself.

▲ We get our vital chemicals from the food we eat. Our plant food is grown with the aid of big agricultural machines such as this one.

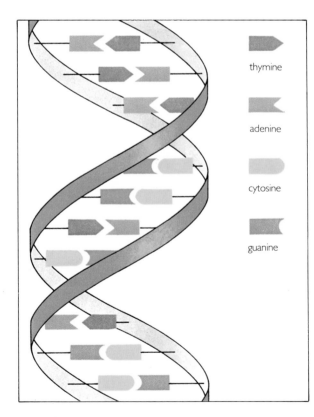

thymine

adenine

cytosine

guanine

◄ DNA is the chemical molecule of heredity (see text). It is a double spiral, built up mainly of the four kinds of smaller chemical molecule. This picture shows only a tiny bit of the whole DNA molecule.

3 THINKING AND DREAMING

BRAIN WAVES AND BODY WAVES

▼ Our feelings – and those of this snarling tiger – are strongly affected by a chemical in our bodies called adrenalin. This is just one of a number of chemical compounds called hormones, which help to control our body and brain waves.

Thoughts, feelings and dreams are the most important things in life, the ones that most vividly show that you are alive. But thoughts, feeling and dreams are not, after all, 'things' in the way that the chemical molecules, gases, liquids and solids mentioned so far in this book are 'things'. On the other hand, thoughts, feelings and dreams do rather resemble waves, rays and other forms of energy.

Thoughts and the brain

Scientists can measure an energy wave or ray. For example, they can find out how many times it vibrates each second, as it moves through space. So can a scientist

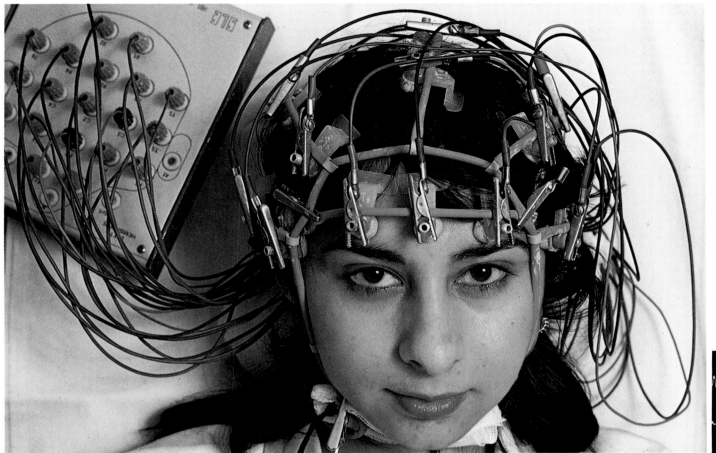

also measure, for example, a thought?

Not exactly, because a thought does not vibrate in space. In fact, a thought cannot be said to exist in space at all. A brain, though, does exist in space. And we know that no thought can exist without the brain to think it. So if a brain somehow does the thinking, then can a scientist somehow measure this process of thinking or 'mental activity'?

The answer here is Yes, because a living brain, whether awake or asleep, gives off electrical energy waves that can be measured very accurately. Also, these waves change their pattern whenever the thinker awakes or falls asleep, or even simply shuts his eyes. These different brain-wave patterns can measure or show, for example, whether a person whose eyes are closed is really asleep or merely pretending.

▲ This girl is connected up to an EEG machine, which measures and records the electrical waves given off by her brain. The results are shown on the **right**.

Body waves

The brain is not the only part of the body to show 'wave behaviour'. Body waves also include rapid electrical waves made by the heart as it beats. Heart waves, like brain waves, can be measured accurately.

Other kinds of body waves, though just as real, are slower and perhaps less easy to measure. For example, your body temperature goes up and down throughout the day and night, in a slow wave or rhythm. Much slower still is the rhythm of a woman's menstruation or bleeding periods. Each of these body waves takes about a whole month.

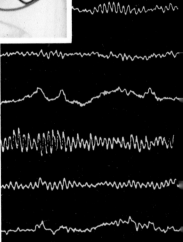

▼ Body waves caused by brain waves. The black wavy line shows movements of a person's eyes when asleep. When the person dreams these eye movements become bigger and faster, as shown by the red wavy line.

SLEEP AND DREAMS

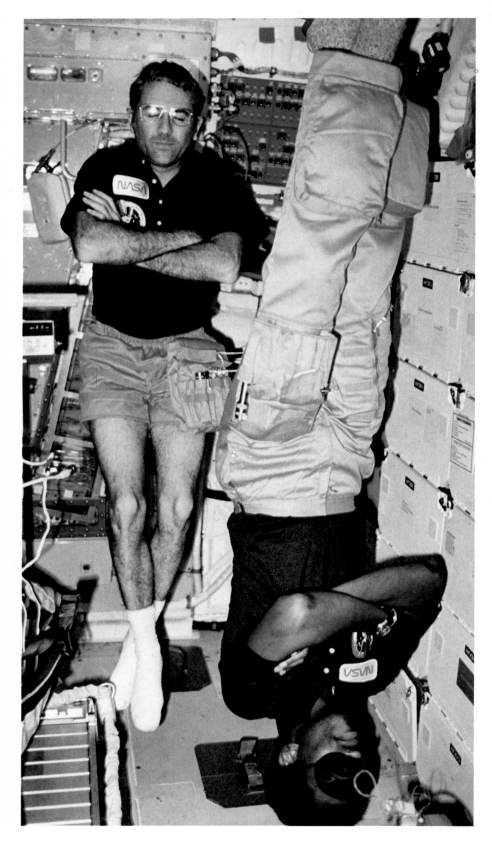

▲ Question: Which of the astronauts is sleeping the right way up? Answer: There is no 'right way up' in space orbit – gravity does not exist as it does here on Earth, so both astronauts are sleeping 'right way up'.

Sleep is very much a part of life. Altogether we spend more than a third of our lives sleeping. A baby or a cat will spend even more of its time asleep – perhaps two thirds of its entire living time. Obviously, sleeping must be very important to us, otherwise we would not spend so much time doing it.

Mysterious sleep

But strangely enough, no-one really knows just why we have to sleep. To get rest after working, yes – but we can rest our bodies and minds in other ways, without becoming unconscious in sleep. To forget our worries? This sounds a good idea – but even people who seem to have no worries usually need their regular eight or so hours of sleep. Worry, in fact, tends to keep us awake rather than send us to sleep.

So sleep is mysterious. All the same, it *is* vitally necessary to nearly all of us. If we are kept without sleep for night after night (as happens to the prisoners of some governments that practise torture) we become very ill and eventually, if not allowed to sleep at all, we will die.

Just occasionally someone is born who needs little sleep, or even no sleep at all. The completely sleepless people are, however, very rare indeed. They only make sleep all the more mysterious, because if *they* can do without it, why is it so vital to all the rest of us?

Dreaming life

When we are asleep, our minds are not just blank and inactive. During dreaming, our minds may be just as active as during the busiest parts of our waking life. Also, have you ever noticed that occasionally you know more or less what is going on around you, even though you know you are asleep?

Your mind is very active when you dream, and this is shown by rapid movements of your eyes. Someone looking at you closely while you are asleep will see your eyelids begin to flicker, as your eyes move from side to side beneath them. Scientists call this *REM* sleep.

If you are then woken up, you will

◄ Curled into a tight little ball, the dormouse sleeps the deep sleep called hibernation. It wakes up only after long intervals, to take a nibble from a nut.

◄ Bats sleep in the position they carry out most of their non-hunting activities – upside down.

◄ Flamingoes asleep– yet they still manage to balance on one leg!

47

▶ Dr Sigmund Freud, shown here with his young wife Martha, wrote a famous book explaining the meaning of dreams. Not all Freud's ideas on dreams are accepted today, but he gave the first believable explanation of the unconscious or dreaming mind.

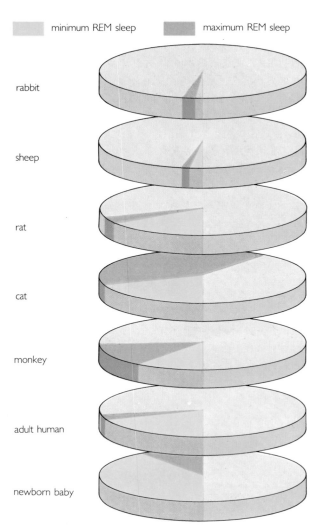

minimum REM sleep   maximum REM sleep

rabbit

sheep

rat

cat

monkey

adult human

newborn baby

▲ How much do animals dream? The pie charts show how much in one whole day, for various animals, including ourselves. REM means Rapid Eye Movements – which are measured to show when a person or animal is dreaming.
▼ We spend a lot of our life sleeping and dreaming. This chart shows how much in a single night.

immediately remember the dream that you were having. Scientists have measured these rapid eye movements of dreamers, and they look like a kind of flickering graph. This is another example of a body wave – but it is also a mind wave as well.

In the morning, after a normal night's sleep (not interrupted by interfering scientists!) you may also remember something of what was going on in your last dream. The dream, though, fades rapidly, so that a minute or two later you have probably forgotten it. Because of this rapid loss of memory, you always forget more of your dreams than you remember.

But this is the same as saying that you always dream more than you think you do. Who can remember dreaming for as long as two hours during a night's sleep? Yet this is the ordinary nightly period of dreaming, as measured by the scientists observing rapid eye movements.

How long is a dream? The answer is that dreams, like motion pictures or TV programmes, vary a great deal in length. They may be 'shorts' lasting only a few minutes. Or they may be full-length

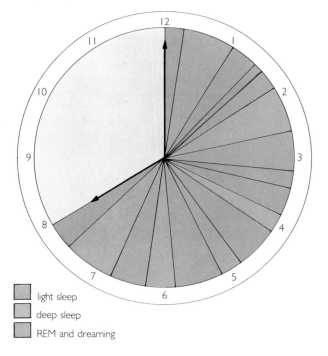

light sleep

deep sleep

REM and dreaming

features lasting up to an hour. This means that you have at least two or three dreams each night. What a waste, not to be able to remember them all!

Deep sleep

Does your brain, then, ever really rest? Yes, because between dreams, your sleep becomes deeper and apparently dreamless. Your brain waves become slower and your eye movements slower and fainter. Other parts of your body also become more peaceful. Your muscles relax and your breathing grows deeper and more regular. Even your body temperature relaxes or goes down a bit.

During the six hours or so of this deep sleep you get each night, your mind and body really do get some relief from all the activity of a busy day—and from dreaming!

▲ Lions, like domestic cats, spend a large part of the day asleep. This lioness will wake up mainly to feed her cubs or to do some hunting.

▼ Dreams often seem so vivid to us while we are having them, but fade quickly when we wake. Throughout the ages artists have tried to recapture vanished dreams. This picture, 'The Dream', by Franz Marc is one example.

WHO'S INTELLIGENT?

Intelligence, power and success

If you are asked for the name of the most powerful of all living creatures, you might answer 'the elephant' or 'a whale'. In one way, you would be correct, because these are among the largest and strongest of all forms of life. But human beings catch and tame elephants and, unfortunately, kill a lot of whales. So human beings are really more powerful than these huge creatures. Their power over the rest of the animal kingdom comes from their extra intelligence.

Because of this superior intelligence, people are the most successful of all the larger animals. Success in the natural world is measured by numbers, and there are many more human beings in the world than any other animals of similar or larger size. All the elephants in the world, for example, number only a few

millions – and many of these live in zoos, under the control of human beings. By contrast, people now number more than 4,000 millions, so that they completely dominate most parts of the Earth's surface. If intelligence can mean all this power and success, then it is worth looking at in more detail.

Brains and intelligence

Where does the mysterious power of intelligence come from? The answer is pretty obvious: the brain. The larger the brain the more intelligent the animal. Human beings, of course, have the largest brains. Or do they? Well, not quite: in fact, some whales and dolphins have larger brains than ours. These are very intelligent animals too, but it is difficult for us to tell just how intelligent they are. They do not speak our language, and we cannot understand enough of theirs to know just how much they can say to one another.

▼ A shark such as this one is a fast and ferocious killer that strikes terror into its often bigger-brained prey, such as the coral fishes it may devour over this tropical reef.

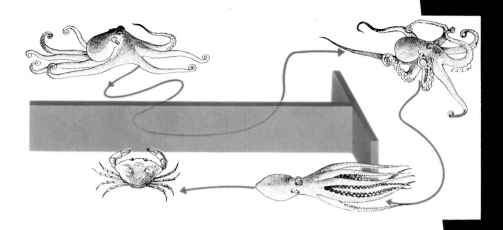

◀ Octopuses feed on crabs. The keen eyes of this octopus have spotted the crab on the other side of the purple glass 'maze'. The octopus's big brain tells it how to find its way round the maze to get at the crab.

▼ Bears, like their cousins the dogs, are intelligent animals. They can be taught to do tricks and were used in circuses for many centuries.

A dolphin is very unlike ourselves. It is shaped very differently, and its life out at sea is totally different from our land-based way of life. It is these great differences that make it difficult for us to measure the dolphin's actual intelligence.

Those other very brainy animals, the great apes, are much more like ourselves, so that we can measure their intelligence rather more exactly. You can see one way in which this is done from the picture (page 53) of the chimpanzee and its picture-language.

The beginnings of intelligence

So far we have considered rather clever animals such as chimps, dolphins and people. But intelligence, and the power that goes with it, began long before any of these brainy creatures was around on the face of the Earth.

Around a hundred million years ago, the biggest and most powerful land animals were certain kinds of dinosaurs – huge reptiles that lived long before mammals such as chimps and dolphins. Dinosaurs were certainly less intelligent than these, but they did have enough brains (and muscle and armour and teeth!) to dominate the Earth at that time.

Go back much farther still, and there comes a time, about 500 million years ago, when animals had not yet left the seas, rivers and lakes to live on land. The world's dominant animals then included the earliest kinds of sharks. These powerful hunters of the sea, many sorts of which still live today, are not very intelligent.

A shark's thinking brain is very small. Most of its brain is taken up with the

◀ Elephants are highly intelligent animals. They were used in the forests of India and south-east Asia to move timber, as they are doing here, long before heavy machinery was invented to do the work.

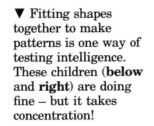

◄ These children's drawings show how you get more expert at putting down what you see on paper. When you are 2 or 3 years old, you will draw a person like the balloon-and-stick-man on the left. But by the age of 8 or 9 you can draw a quite real-looking person such as the one on the right.

▼ Fitting shapes together to make patterns is one way of testing intelligence. These children (**below** and **right**) are doing fine – but it takes concentration!

► A game for the very intelligent – chess in a park in Zurich in Switzerland.

► Sarah, this young female chimpanzee, has been taught a simple language. Its 'words' are the coloured shapes. Sarah reads the shapes-sentence on the left, which tells her to put the apple in the bucket and the banana in the dish. As a prize for being such a clever chimp, she is then allowed to eat the apple and banana!

	Sarah
	Mary
	bucket
	dish
	apple
	banana
	is
	give
	put
	different
	no-not
	?
	red
	yellow
	brown

sense of smell. It is mainly by this sense that a shark follows and searches out its prey, until it gets quite close, when its eyes guide it to a swift and savage attack. Since the shark does not seem to think much, if at all, about this hunting process, it could almost be called 'a hunting machine'.

Automatic behaviour

More usually we say that animals such as sharks, with small brains, show automatic behaviour. That is, such animals always do the same things in the same circumstances. They do not have the intelligence to vary their behaviour, and so to do different things sometimes.

As well as big animals such as sharks, many other smaller kinds of animal show automatic behaviour. All insects, for example, always behave in exactly the same way in the same circumstances. This is why you can usually catch a fly if you try hard enough – the fly does not have the intelligence to do something different and escape. But even non-

intelligent animals can have power. Sharks still dominate parts of the seas, and until recently, parts of Africa were virtually ruled by billions of disease-carrying tsetse flies!

▼ When a tsetse fly pierces skin to feed on blood, it can inject the deadly microbes of the disease called sleeping sickness.

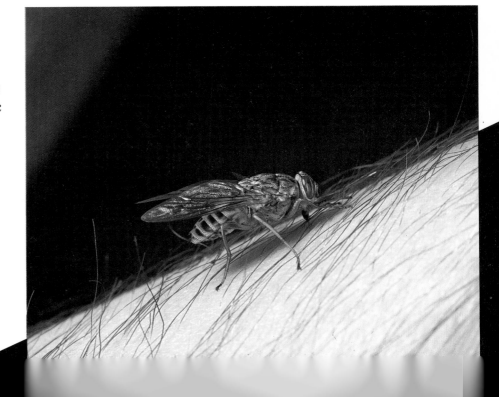

ALL BY INSTINCT

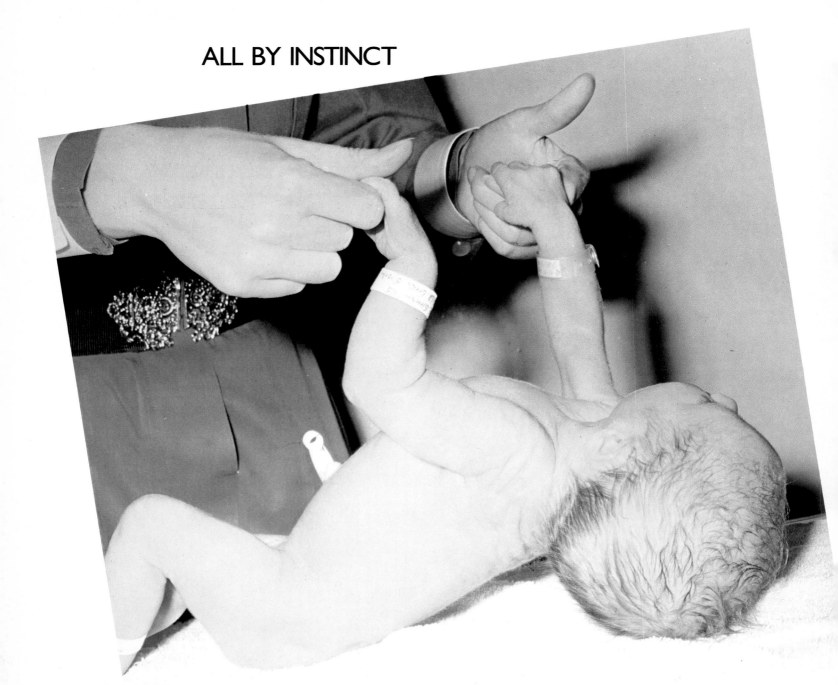

▲ A newborn baby's instinct tells it to hold tight to mother (here, a nurse). This instinct is a leftover from very ancient times, when a baby had to hang on to its mother's hair or fur as she roamed about gathering food.

The flies and the sharks described on page 53 are non-intelligent animals that show automatic behaviour. They always do the same thing in the same circumstances. But of course, even highly intelligent creatures such as ourselves also show a good deal of automatic behaviour.

Sometimes this automatic behaviour is pretty trivial. Have you ever caught yourself scratching your head, when puzzled? At other times, automatic behaviour can be very useful. If a ball or a piece of grit flies towards your eyes,

these shut quickly and automatically. You do not think first about protecting yourself – this would take too long for safety.

So automatic behaviour can be important. In the case of the non-intelligent shark, its nose leads it automatically towards food. In the case of highly-intelligent you, your eyelids shut down automatically to protect your eyes.

Born behaviour
Actions such as these, which we *must* do first, and think about only later, are called reflex actions. The newborn baby in the picture grasps the nurse's fingers quite automatically. If it was a baby

◀ A swarm of bees is an impressive sight. These bees are starting a new colony. This demands exact forms of instinctual behaviour to succeed.

▲ Ants must co-operate in order to move particles as large as the one shown. This seems very like intelligence, yet the ants are behaving entirely by instinct.

▼ The chicks' instinct tells them to gape widely when either parent bird arrives at the nest. The sight of their gaping beaks makes the parent release the food it has gathered, to feed the chicks. So there are two instincts at work here.

◀ Grayling leaping a small waterfall. River fishes often behave in this manner to reach the quiet places in the river where they spawn (lay their eggs). They swim upstream entirely by instinct, to find these places.

monkey or ape, it would need to grasp tightly to stay clinging to its mother's body as she climbed or ran.

Do you know any other reflexes? Here is a well-known one. Cross one leg on the knee of the other, then tap your outside knee. Your leg will jerk quite automatically, without you being able to stop it. There is no very obvious reason for this reflex action.

Living by instinct

As well as these simple automatic reflex actions, there is more complicated automatic behaviour. Bees, ants and wasps lead very complicated lives, in which hundreds or thousands of the insects live in the same nest and do dozens of different jobs – all quite automatically. We say that these social insects, like the shark, live not by thinking but by *instinct*.

Once again, though, we ourselves live at least partly by instinct. Our best-known instinct is our sex instinct. When boys and girls reach the age of puberty, their behaviour changes a lot, particularly with regard to the opposite sex – and they often wonder why.

HAVING VISIONS

Mostly, you believe that what you see really exists. Otherwise, you say to yourself, I wouldn't see it. Really, though, you quite often see things that are 'not there'. Remember your dreams – they are full of visible objects and people that are not there, except in your imagination.

Even when you are wide awake, you may see something that is not there. As in dreams, this can happen by imagination – pictures behind your closed eyelids, and so on. Usually you take these for granted – they are just 'mental pictures'. Sometimes, though, it can happen when your eyes are wide open – and then you begin to wonder.

Scientific visions

Seeing something that is not there can have a scientific explanation. Nearly everyone has seen a mirage at some time. A mirage is a vision of something – usually a sheet of water on a hot day – that is not there, but is caused by the bending of light. When light rays from the Sun pass from colder upper air to hotter air near the ground, they bend, and so carry a picture of the sky to your eyes – this is the 'sheet of water' you see.

UFOs, or Unidentified Flying Objects, are more of a scientific puzzle. Sensible, practical people such as airplane pilots

▲ Can a ghost be photographed? This picture seems to show that it can. The ghost in question is known as The Brown Lady of Raynam Hall, in Norfolk, England.

▶ The ancient Greeks believed that the supreme powers were the Fates, which both humans and gods had to obey. Here they are showing the body of Queen Clytemnestra to her son Orestes, who murdered her.

▼ Scenes from a haunting. In the top three pictures the two girls are removed from bed by an unknown force. One of the girls is often found asleep on a large radio without knowing how she got there. In the bottom picture, an investigator resists a force lifting the sleeping girl's body. Are the forces normal ones – examples of the girl's own muscle power? Or are they paranormal, poltergeist forces?

sometimes report having seen one of these. Often it is something disk-shaped, whirling or otherwise moving fast through the air. Is it a visiting spaceship from another planet? Or is it an unusual whirling air movement that just looks similar to a spaceship? Until a UFO actually lands, and someone or something gets out of it, we may never know for certain.

Troubled visions

Other wide-awake visions trouble us more, not only because we cannot explain them scientifically, but also they seem more personal and threatening to us. Hallucinations are visions of things that are really in our minds, but which we have projected outwards, so that we see them as though they were outside us.

Ghosts may or may not be one kind of hallucination. They certainly are very unscientific visions, but even in modern times this has not stopped people seeing them. Also scary are poltergeists. These invisible spirits or powers are said to make objects such as chairs, tables and vases move around in a noisy and aggressive fashion. Like ghosts, their existence has not been proved.

MIND POWER

In this book we have considered many of the invisible forces or powers in the Universe. These include the force of gravity, and forces in atoms, including chemical forces. We have also mentioned mental force, or mind power. Poltergeists, or ghostly movers of things, seem to be one strange result of the power of the human mind. But not everyone believes in poltergeists. So does mental force really exist, in the way that the force of gravity or atomic forces exist?

Telepathy and PK

The force of gravity acts over great distances – right across the Universe, in fact. Other forms of energy can travel in waves or rays over long distances (pages 20 to 23). So what about mental energy – can this also travel about, to exert a mind force or power?

One way in which 'mind waves' possibly travel is from one mind to another, so that someone's thoughts appear in someone else's head. This is called telepathy, or 'thinking at a distance'. A few people, for example, can guess the identity of playing cards or other pictures being looked at by another person in another place. More often, though, telepathy seems to happen by accident, when someone just 'gets a message' from someone else, perhaps unknown.

Another form of mind power is power over distant things. This force is known as *psychokinesis*, or PK for short. One form of PK, as with poltergeists, causes

▲ The eye of Horus (**top**), and the key-like object called the Ankh (**above**), are two symbols often used by the ancient Egyptians to ward off the power of evil.

▼ This photograph claims to show the power of mind over the force of gravity, during meditation. But there are clever ways of altering photographs, so that you wouldn't notice ...

► The famous Indian rope trick. When the climber reaches the top, he silently vanishes ...

◀ This nail-sitter has hypnotized himself so that he feels little or no discomfort from the nails on which he is sitting.

▼ Hypnotism first became famous in the 18th century. It was said to cure many diseases, which it certainly did not.

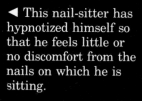

distant things to move. A gambler, for example, may use PK to cause the dice or cards he is playing with to fall or come out lucky for him. Actually, such gambling power is not very effective and may be quite imaginary – although some people *do* seem to have a small power to 'influence' dice and playing cards. Another form of PK is still more mysterious. Uri Geller became famous for being able to bend spoons by mind power. Some other people have claimed to be able to make clouds disappear by 'thinking them away'.

Lots and lots of minds

Perhaps most of these examples of mind power seem rather small and unimportant. Who wants to bend spoons or guess playing cards anyway? Still, if mind power is as 'real' as gravity or atomic forces, then it must be very important. Remember, there are more than 4,000 million human minds on our world alone. And the Universe contains countless billions of other worlds …

▲ Uri Geller became famous because he could apparently bend metal objects by using the power of his mind. Here he indicates a fork that he has just bent.

► The power of mind over pain and fear is shown by these fire walkers in south-east Asia.

Alloys are hard substances made up of one or more kinds of metal, with perhaps other, non-metallic substances also. Steel, brass and aluminium alloys are examples.

Atoms are the smallest parts of any **chemical element** that we can say still 'are' that element. For example, a single atom of the gas hydrogen will still have all the properties of that gas, but anything smaller will not. For what atoms themselves are made up of, see **Sub-atomic particles**.

Chemical compounds are substances made up of two or more kinds of chemical element bonded or linked together. If they are not bonded but just mixed, then the substance is not a chemical compound but a mixture.

Chemical elements are the simplest kinds of substances. They are made up of only one kind of atom. There are 92 different chemical elements in nature, and so 92 different kinds of atom. About 15 more chemical elements can be made by scientists—these are called artificial elements.

Chemical reactions happen whenever one kind of chemical substance changes into another. When a metal dissolves in an acid, this is a chemical reaction. Other, more complicated chemical reactions happen in the bodies of living creatures—for example, when we digest our food, or when a green plant makes its own food from the carbon dioxide gas of the air.

Chloroplasts are tiny living packets that give the leaves and stems of plants their green appearance. This green is due to chlorophyll. With the aid of the chlorophyll in their chloroplasts, together with sunlight, green plants make their own body-substances from the carbon dioxide gas of the air.

Crystals are hard substances with a very regular shape. Gemstones are the most familiar crystals but many other substances are also crystalline, although their crystals may be too small to be seen without a microscope. Crystals have such a regular shape because their **atoms** are arranged very regularly.

Electro-magnets have much more magnetic power or force than ordinary magnets. They are made by passing an electric current through a metal wire coiled around an iron bar.

Enzymes are chemical substances that make the **chemical reactions** of life happen. They are found, for example, in our blood. Enzymes are special kinds of the very complicated chemical molecules called proteins. Other proteins include the ones that make up the muscles of our bodies.

Focus is the coming-together of rays of light or other kinds of wave-energy. You can focus light and heat rays from the Sun easily enough with a magnifying glass, to set a bit of paper or straw on fire. X-rays and other penetrating rays can also be focussed with special machines.

Galaxy is the name of the great cloud of stars, dust and gas that contains our own Sun and its planets. As well as our own galaxy, the **Universe** also contains countless other galaxies, each containing a huge number of stars.

Instincts are those sorts of responses that we, or other animals, are born with, and so do not have to learn. A newborn baby will turn its head to its mother's breast and suck milk from it without ever having been taught to do so. A shark lives mostly by instinct – nearly all its actions are unlearned.

Molecule is the term used to describe a group of **atoms** of a substance that are linked or bonded together. A molecule of common salt has one atom of the metal sodium bonded to one atom of the gas chlorine. A molecule of the gas hydrogen has two hydrogen atoms linked together. A molecule of the gas helium is rather unusual because it consists only of a single atom. Most substances have molecules more complicated than any of these examples, with more atoms in them.

Psychokinesis or PK is a mysterious human power to move or influence objects by thought alone. A gambler may influence the dice he is throwing to fall in lucky ways. A spoon or fork may be bent by 'thought power'. PK may be science – or it may be magic.

REM sleep means Rapid Eye Movement Sleep. When you dream, your eyes move about faster under your closed eyelids. This is how scientists tell that you are dreaming, and measure the length of your dreams.

Sub-atomic particles are particles even smaller than **atoms**. Some sub-atomic particles, such as electrons, are commonly found both inside and outside atoms. Other kinds of sub-atomic particles stay inside atoms most of the time. Atoms, in fact, are made up entirely of various kinds of sub-atomic particles.

Ultraviolet rays come to Earth mostly from the Sun. They are the energy rays in sunlight that turn our skins brown when we sunbathe. Some ultraviolet rays have so much energy that they would kill us. Luckily, these high-energy rays are stopped from reaching our bodies by the Earth's atmosphere or air.

Universe is the name we give to all the substance or matter, and all the energy, there is. Our own Earth and everything on it, is the very tiniest speck in the Universe, which contains countless millions of planets and stars.

Vapour is the name given to a gas that has cooled and turned into tiny droplets of liquid. A morning mist is a vapour, and so is steam from a kettle. These both consist of many tiny droplets of water.

Vitamins are substances in our food that are vital to our health, yet which we need only in very small amounts. Anyone who fails to get even these small amounts of any vitamin, will suffer from a deficiency disease. Such diseases are still common in the poorest countries of the world.

◀ The Aurora Borealis, or Northern Lights, is produced by rays and particles from the Sun, which collide with atoms of the air, causing an electrical glow.

INDEX

Acetylene 34
Acids 36, 37, 43
Airships 9
Antimatter 30
Astronauts 19, 46
Atoms 6, 16, 20, 28–29
Automatic behaviour 53

Bacteria 11
Behaviour
  automatic 53, 54
  born 54–55
Blood cells 11
Body
  chemicals 40–43
  energy 38–39
  waves 45
Boiling 14
Brains
  and intelligence 50–53
  automatic behaviour
    53
  waves 44–45
Brown Lady of Raynam
    Hall, Norfolk 56

Carbon dioxide 10
Chemicals
  body 40–43
  compounds 36, 37
  elements 36
  forces 34–37
  substances 36
Chlorine 36
Chlorophyll 37
Clytemnestra, Queen 56
Coal 24
Compounds, chemical 36,
    37
Compressed air 19
Cosmic rays 22
Crystals 16, 17

DNA 43
Dreams 46, 48, 49
Dynamite 34, 35

Earth forces 32
Electrical
  charge 29
  energy 24, 25
  generator 26
Electricity 26, 27
Electrons 20, 28–29, 32
Emptiness 6
Energy
  chemical 25
  electrical 24, 25
  examples 22
  for life 38–39
  force, see Force
  locked-up 24
  matter into 30
  movement- 26
  non-travelling 24
  quick 38
  slow 38
  sound 26
  stored 26
  travelling 23, 24
  what is 24–25
Enzymes 42, 43
Evil 58

Fates 56
Fire walkers 60–61
Food 38, 43
Force
  chemical 34–35
  cousins 32
  earth 32
  energy and 26–27
  long-distance 29
  magnetic 32
  nuclear 30
  of attraction 28
Freezing 14
Freud, Martha 48
Freud, Dr Sigmund 48

Galaxies 6, 7
Gases
  breathed by humans
    10–11
  common 8
  invisible 8–9
  lightest 8
  molecules 12, 16
  pie chart 8
  space rocket 14–15
  structure 6
  uncommon 8
Geller, Uri 59
Geysers 33
Ghosts 56, 57
Glass 16
Gold 18
Gravity 28, 29, 30,
    58

H-bomb 30, 31, 32
Hallucinations 57
Haunting 57
Heat 22, 24, 33
Heavier 18
Heaviest 18
Helium 8, 9
Hemoglobin 37
Heredity 43
Hydrogen 8, 9, 18
Hypnotism 59

Ice 16
Instinct 54–55
Intelligence 50–53
Iron 32

Krakatoa 32

Light 22
Lightest 18
Liquids
  capillary action 13
  curious habits 12
  molecules 12, 16
  structure 6
  surface-binding force
    12
  what are 12–13
Locomotive 25

Magnesium 37
Magnetism 32
Matter
  into energy 30
  meaning 6
  structure 6
Melting 14
Mercury 18
Metals 18
Milk 12
Milky Way 6
Mind power 58–61
Mineral crystals 17
Molecules
  complicated 37
  meaning 12
  metal 37
  of heredity 43
  protein 40, 42, 43
  simple 37
  solids 16, 20
Moon 8

Nail-sitter 59
Nitrogen 10, 11
Non-crystals 16
Nuclear force 30
Nucleic acids 43

Osmium 18

Oxidation 34, 36
Oxygen 10–11, 34, 36
Ozone 11

Particles 20, 28
Peat 37
Plasma 20
Platinum 18
Poltergeists 57, 58
Power 50
Proteins 40, 42, 43
Psychokinesis 58–59
Pyromorphite 17

REM 46, 48
Radiation 30
Radioactivity 23
Rays 22–23, 24
Rope trick 58
Ruby 16
Rust 34

Salt, 36, 37
Saturn 28
Scientific visions 56–57
Scuba diver 19
Selenium 16
Sex instinct 55
Sky 20
Sleep 46–49
Sodium 36
Solar furnace 25
Solids
  meaning 6
  molecules 16
  structure 6
Sound energy 26
Space 6
Space rocket 14–15
Stars 6, 7, 8, 18, 20
Substances
  changing 34
  chemical 36
  radioactive 23
  super-heavy 18
Sugar 16, 26, 37–39
Sun 9, 10–11, 20, 25

Telepathy 58
Thoughts 44–45
Tokyo 27
Travelling energy 23, 24
Trees 37

Ultraviolet rays 11
Unidentified flying
    objects 56–57
Universe
  atoms and 28–29
  emptiness 6, 7

Vapour 6
Vinegar 36
Visions 56–57
Vitamins 40, 41

Volcano 20, 21, 33

Water
  atoms 24
  boiling 14, 16
  cycle 12–13
  solid 16
Wavellite 17
Waves
  body 45
  brain 44–45
  energy 22–23
  mind 58
  ray 23
Wood 42

X-rays 23, 24

Zinc 16

Acknowledgments

Heather Angel, Ardea,
Associated Press,
Barnaby's Picture
Library, Camera Press,
Charpentier, Nino
Cirani, Bruce Coleman,
G Dagli Orti, © DACS
1985, Daily Telegraph
Colour Library, Mary
Evans Picture Library/
Harry Price Collection,
Mrs EL Freud, A de
Gregario, Roland Haas,
Michael Holford,
Archivio IGDA, JL,
Jacana, M King, Roger
Kohn, A Margiocco,
Marka, Marshall
Cavendish/JJ Mollit,
John Mason, S & D
McCutcheon, R Merlo,
Ken Moreman, Graham
Morris, Brian Mullan,
Museo Civico di Storia
Naturale di Milano,
NASA, NHPA, G
Nimatallah, Oxford
Scientific Films, PAF
International, ME
Parker, Dr Peacock/
Leeds Royal Infirmary,
Photri, Picturepoint, The
Platinum Shop, Royal
Observatory Edinburgh,
Science Photo Library,
Syndication
International, R
Thompson and F Lane, F
Tomasi, John Topham
Library, UKAEA,
United Kingdom Atomic
Energy Authority, World
Government of the Age of
Enlightenment.